Eye-Pleasing, Mind-Teasing 3-D Conundrums

Eye-Pleasing, Mind-Teasing 3-D Conundrums

László Kresz

Károly Kresz

István Kresz

With a foreword by

László Mérõ

STERLING PUBLISHING CO., INC.
New York

Library of Congress Cataloging-in-Publication Data Available

2   4   6   8   10   9   7   5   3

Published by Sterling Publishing Co., Inc.
387 Park Avenue South, New York, NY 10016
Originally published in Hungary under the title
Látványos Logika: Térbeli logikai rejvények szemfüleseknek
and © 2001 by István Kresz, Károly Kresz, and László Kresz.
English translation © 2003 by Sterling Publishing Co., Inc.
Distributed in Canada by Sterling Publishing
ᶜ/o Canadian Manda Group, One Atlantic Avenue, Suite 105
Toronto, Ontario, Canada M6K 3E7
Distributed in Great Britain by Chrysalis Books
64 Brewery Road, London N7 9NT, England
Distributed in Australia by Capricorn Link (Australia) Pty. Ltd.
P.O. Box 704, Windsor, NSW 2756, Australia

Sterling ISBN 1-4027-0554-9

CONTENTS

Bright people err smarter than other people are right.

Just one example: Esther Dyson, the famous Internet guru, postulated that the Internet would become basically free and would be maintained by advertisements. So many smart people would use it so much, advertisers would happily fall all over it.

This idea was subjected to criticism from the time of its birth. It has been calculated that Internet development requires as much money as the total advertising budget of the entire world, and television and print news media compete with the Internet for ad revenues. Advertising, this other point of view claimed, would not be able to maintain the Internet. And that turned out to be true. In April 2000, the colossal collapse of the stock exchange loudly proclaimed the downfall of Esther Dyson's opinion.

Yet, the Internet has developed so much, it has become an integral part of our life, and it is beginning to maintain itself in its own right. What's more, it would not have come about without Esther Dyson's mistake and would not have developed at such an accelerated pace. Esther Dyson, a really smart person, erred smarter and more constructively than her critics were right.

How does someone become smart? I would not say that busily solving puzzles like the ones in this book is the only way. First of all, you must enjoy solving puzzles for them to contribute the most to your intelligence-building. Formal education helps build intelligence, but sometimes it can also get in the way. If someone is capable of becoming a smart person, his or her mind must be continuously nourished, but not just with heavy reading and problems.

For thousands of years, puzzles have kept people's minds awake and provided them with nourishment and stimulation. Just as spices can perk up the experience of eating, puzzles add interest and excitement to the process of becoming smarter and can make learning more appealing and fun.

It is good to think. More accurately: it is good to think in moderation. Similarly, drinking and mountain-climbing are also good in moderation. Many of us are fond of climbing the occasional hill, but few climb the Himalayas—most of us would not survive it. The beauty of good puzzles is that they require much thinking, are fun, and the joy of solving the puzzle makes the time well worth the effort. Athletic activity, if done in moderation, can make our bodies healthier and reward us with the joy of performance; puzzles can give our mind and brain healthy development, stamina, and endurance.

The puzzles in this book continue the tradition of millennia but are truly products of the 21st century. The puzzlemaker, computer programmer, and graphic artist have all made important contributions to the creativity you will find in these pages. Classic ideas and puzzles were given not only new and modern form but were also improved. New technical possibilities inspired new puzzle concepts.

Why are new puzzles needed? Isn't the development from the sphinx to Ernõ Rubik enough? While we seek wisdom from the ancient world, we always need new work that reflects modern life. This book succeeds beautifully at presenting both the old and the new in the most modern wrapping.

—László Mérõ
Budapest, Hungary

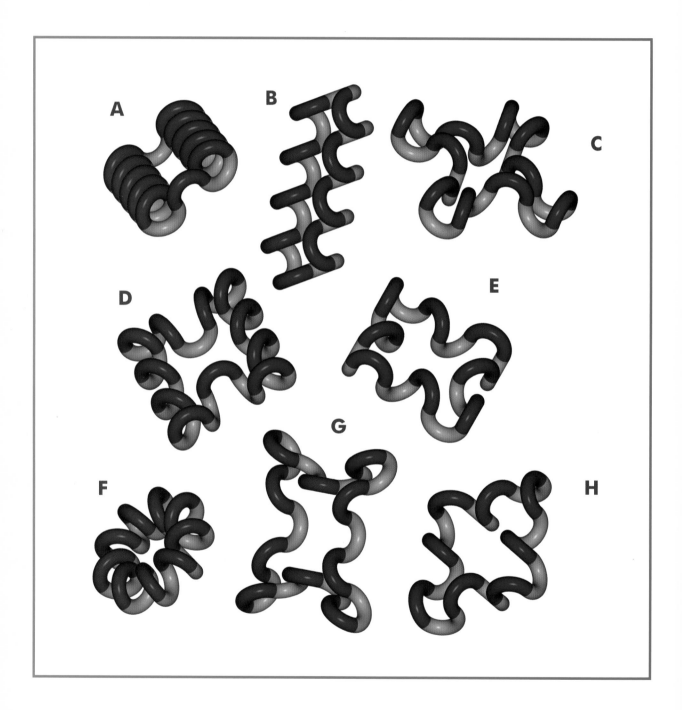

The structures marked with letters are built from the four shapes on the right. Which shape reaches downward the farthest if the red and yellow horizontal rod is removed?

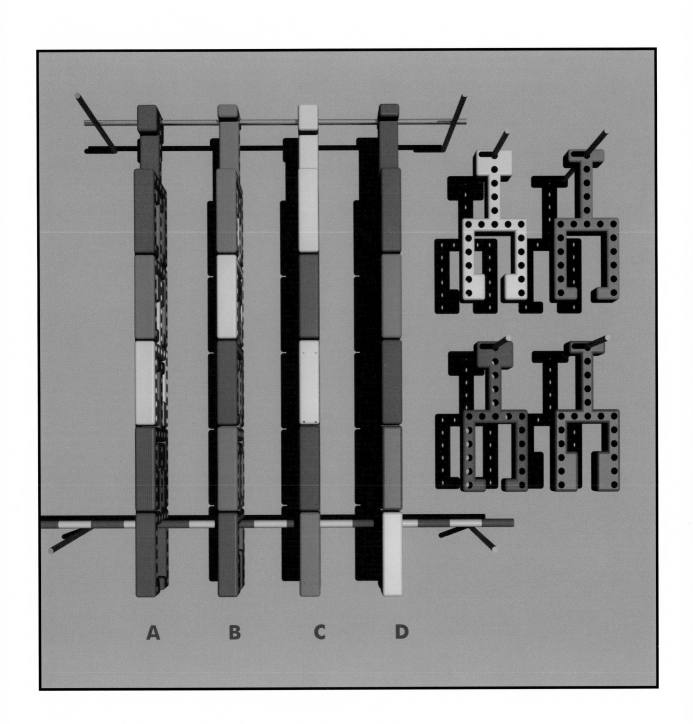

The sum of the numbers on the top of the dice is 8 greater than the sum of those on the bottom. The sum of the numbers on the top and bottom of each die is 7. What number is on the bottom of the lowest die?

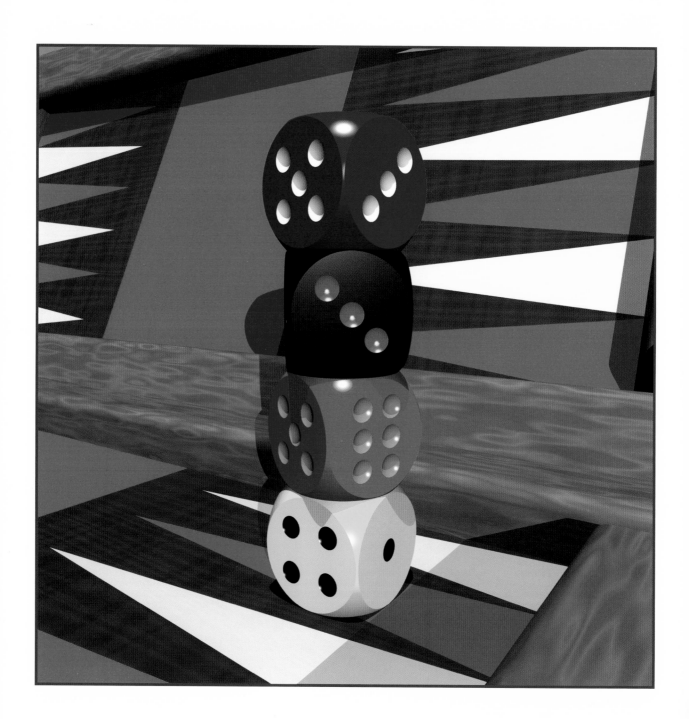

Which string of pearls contains the longest uninterrupted black-and-white sequence?

A

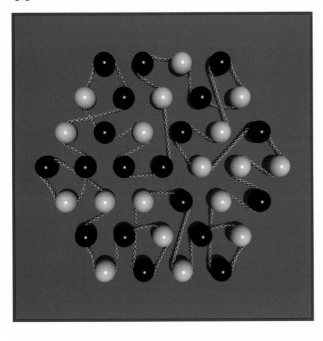

B

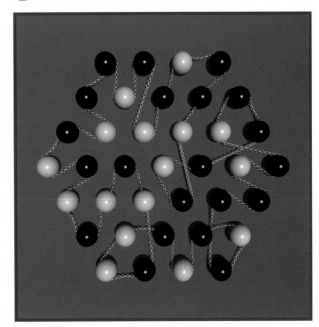

C

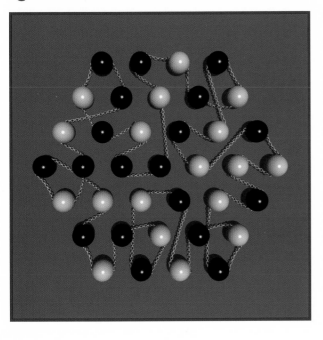

D

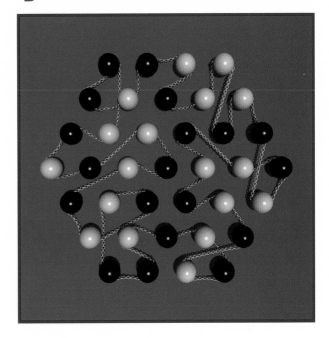

5 Combine the crosses and the squiggles to create a pattern similar to the one shown in the center box so each line is enclosed by a squiggle.

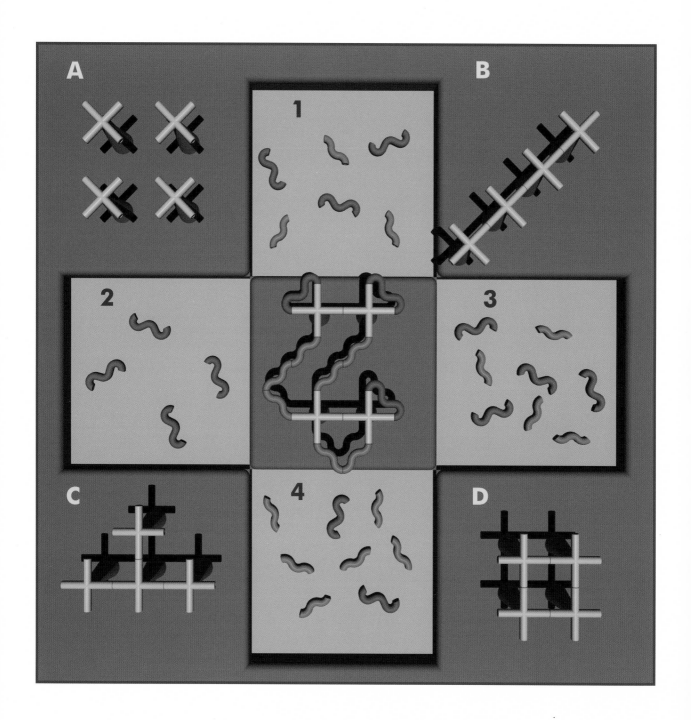

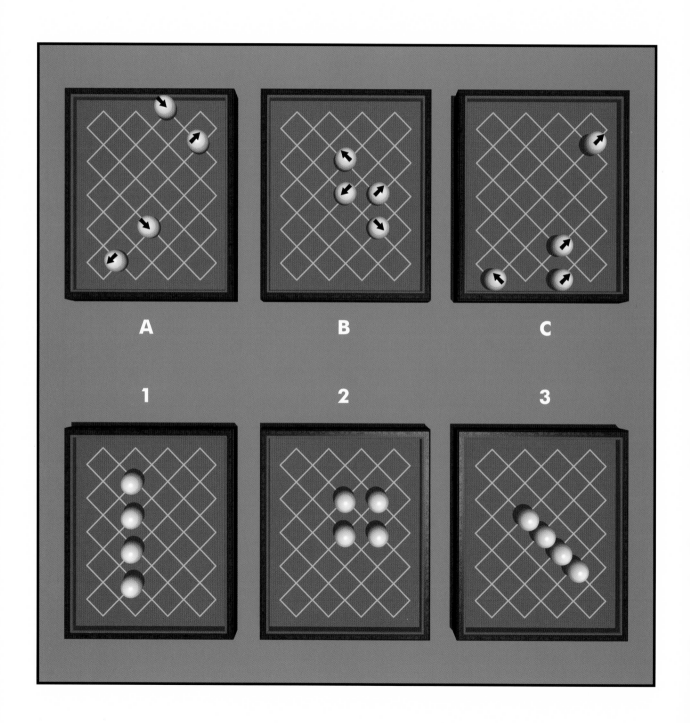

8   In what order did we stack up the shapes?

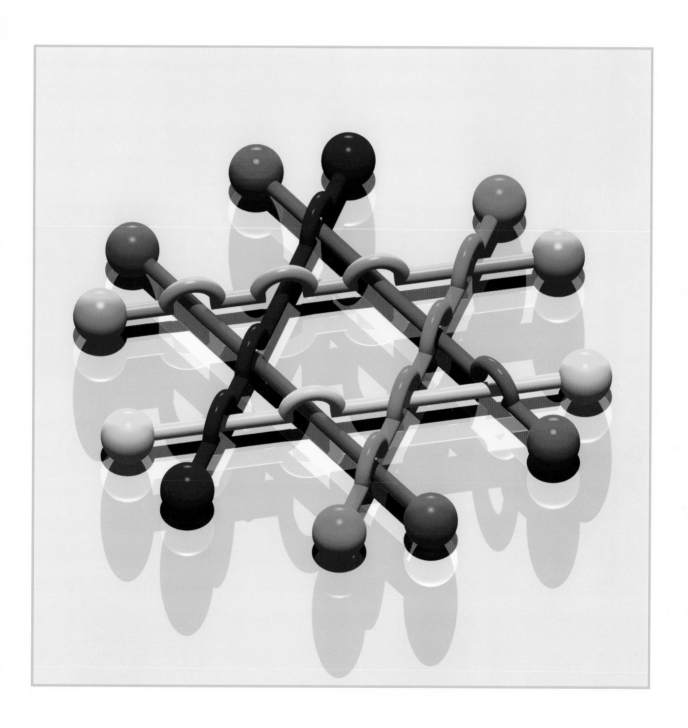

Pair the shapes with their shadows.

1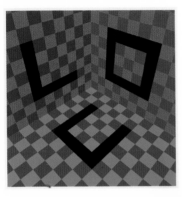

2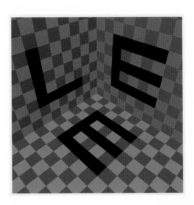

3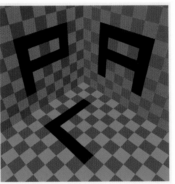

4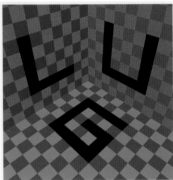

A

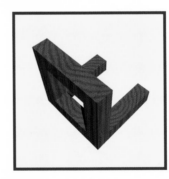

B

C

D

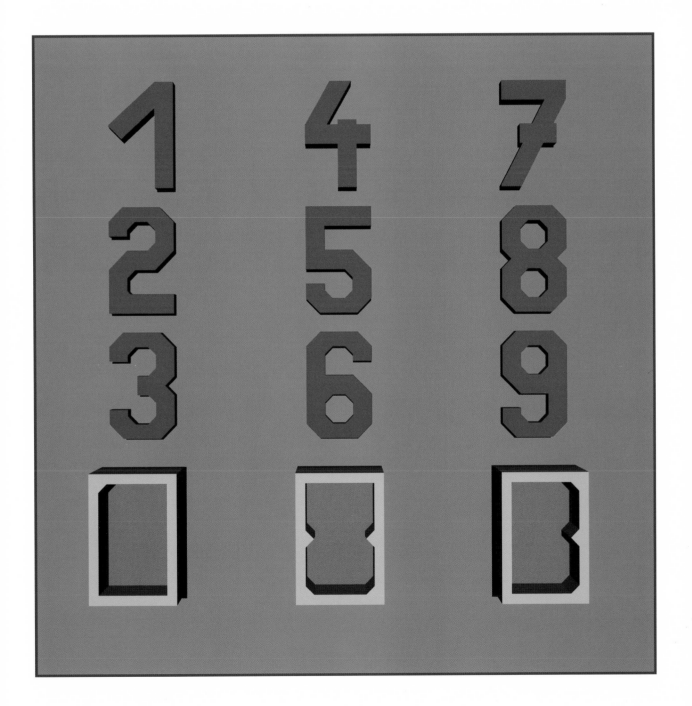

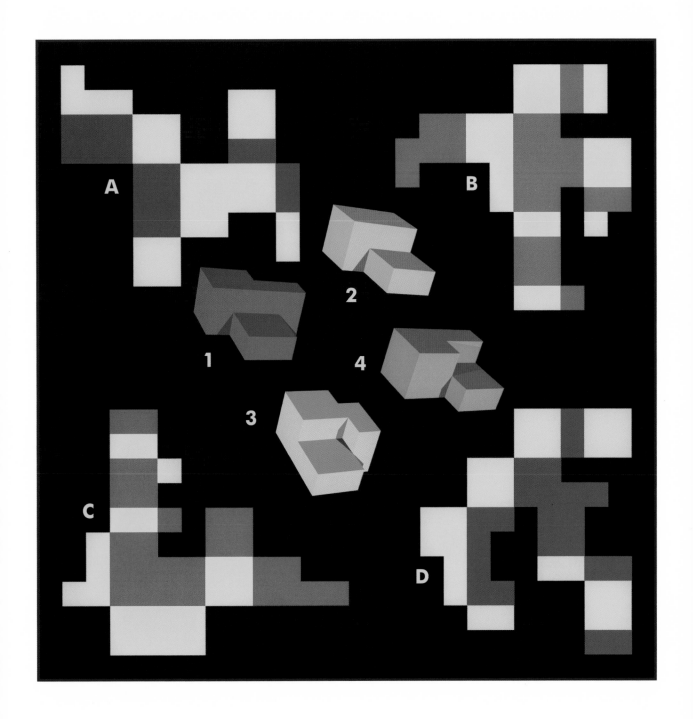

How many separate ribbons have been woven into one?

Pair up the ends of the ribbons.

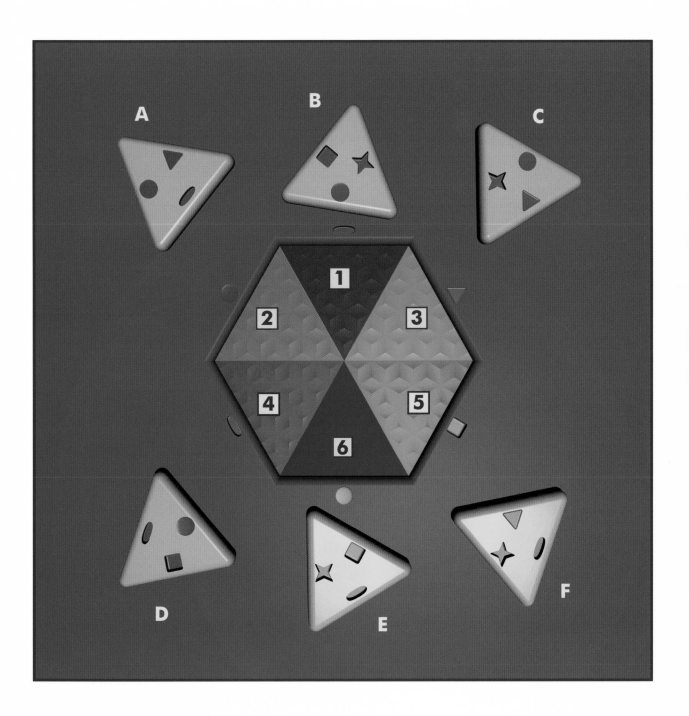

17 By pairing the shapes below, you can assemble large cubes each containing 27 smaller cubes.

A

B

C
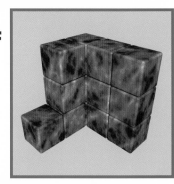

D
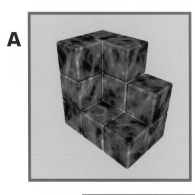

E
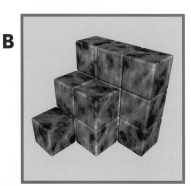

F

G
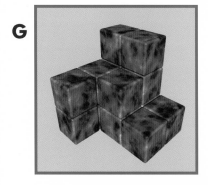

H
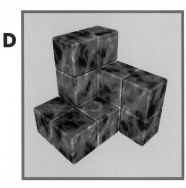

I
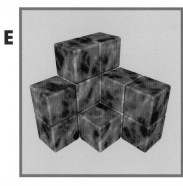

J
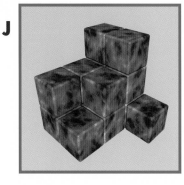

K

L
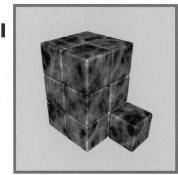
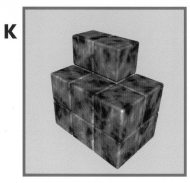
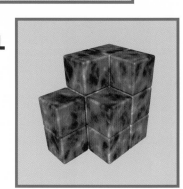

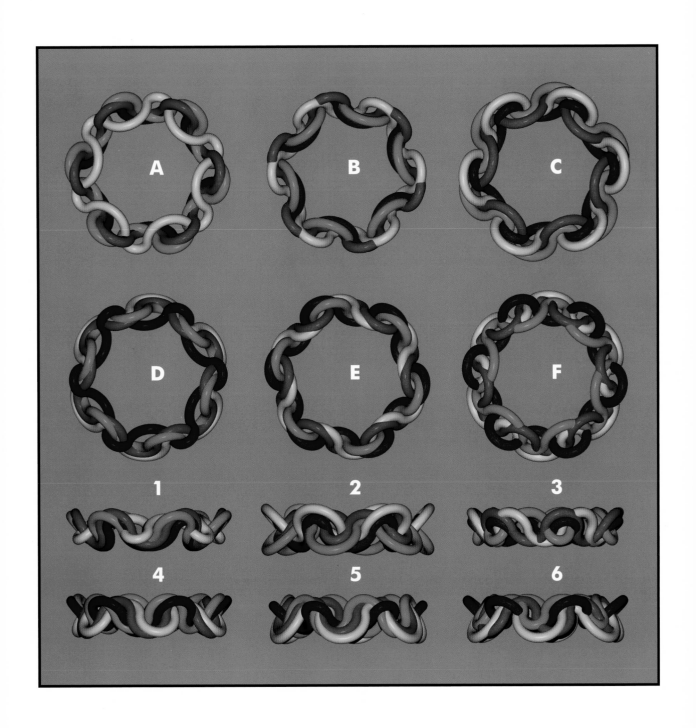

19 Which pairs of shapes should be merged to create the structures at the bottom?

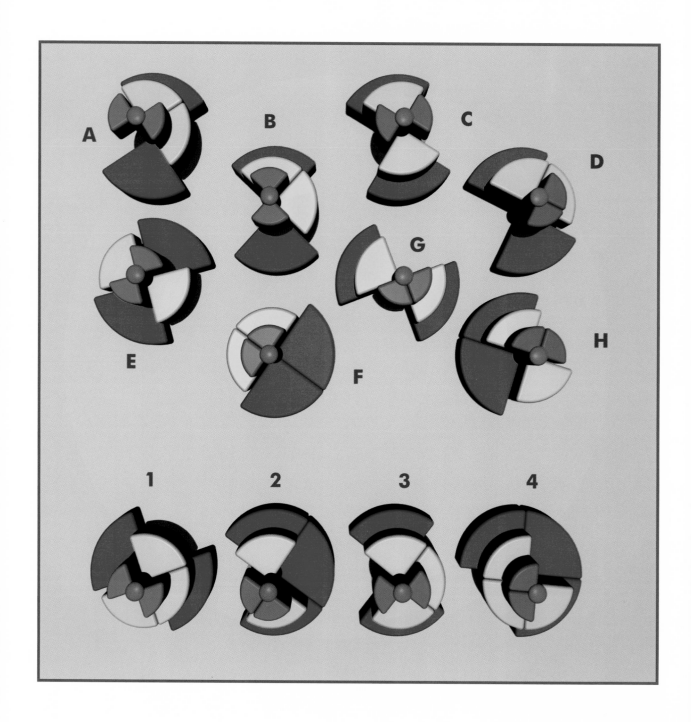

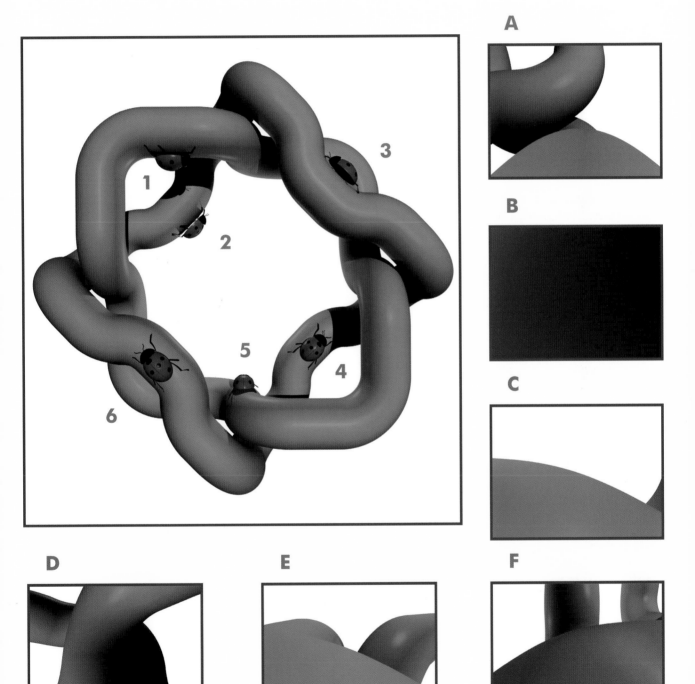

A

B

C

D

E

F

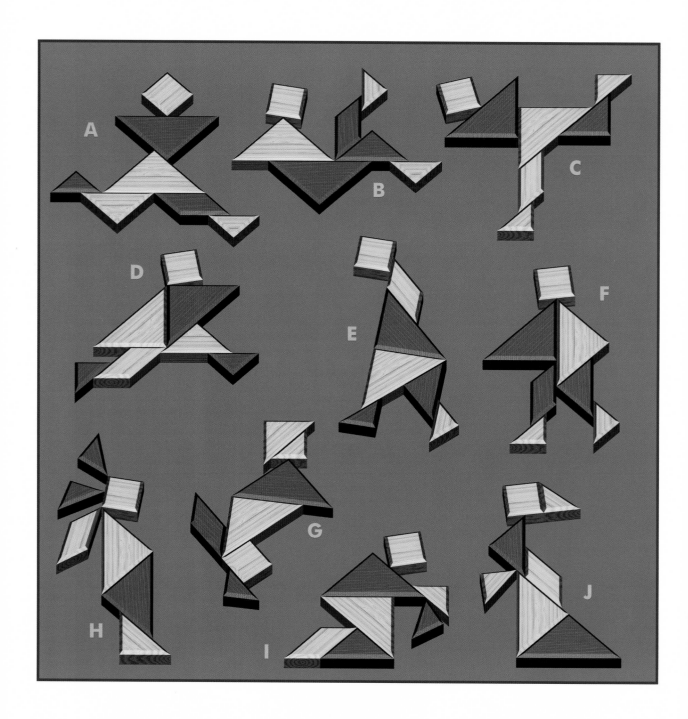

A

B

C

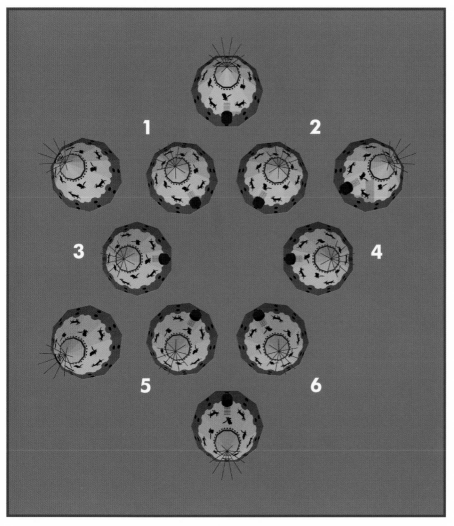

D

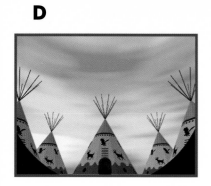

E

F

The magic cube shown in the upper left corner has been rearranged. In each step, we turned one of the outer faces 90 degrees. Put the pictures in order.

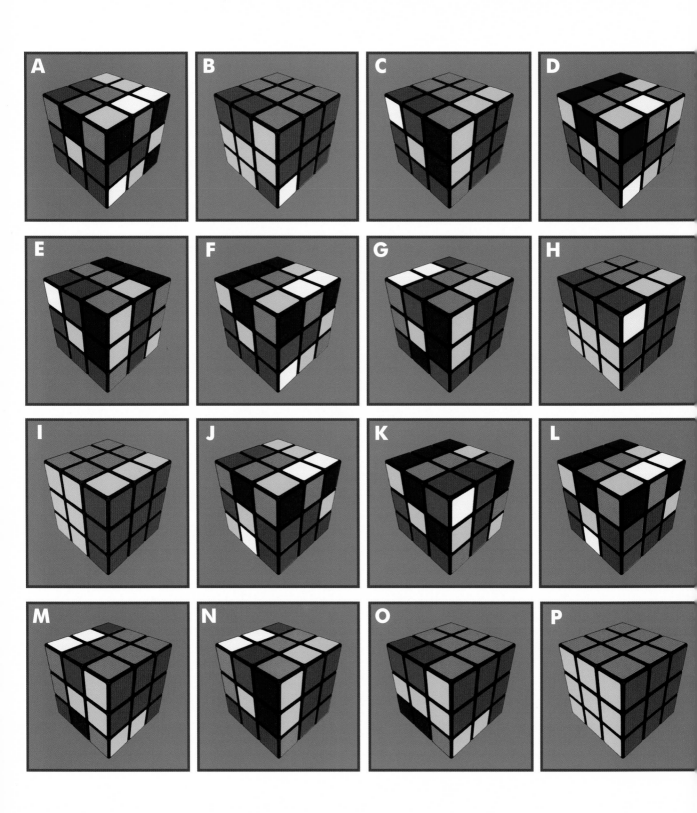

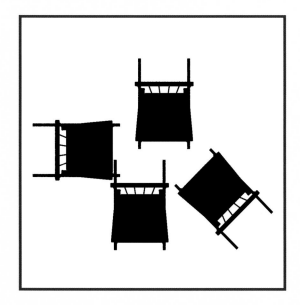

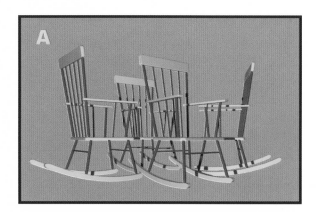

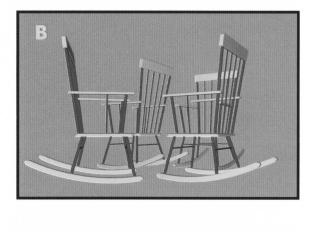

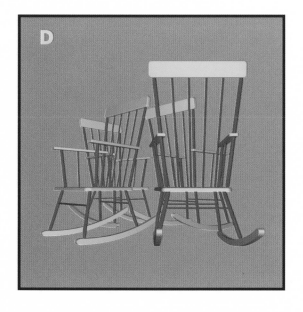

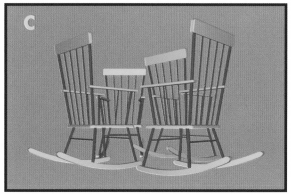

Each light is controlled by one of the switches, but we don't know which, and we don't know the on and the off positions of the switches. Study the first three pictures and guess which lights are on in the fourth one.

1

2

3

4

The four small monsters ramble along in their labyrinths at the same speed. They never turn back and they gobble up every circle along the way. Which vertical column will be emptied first?

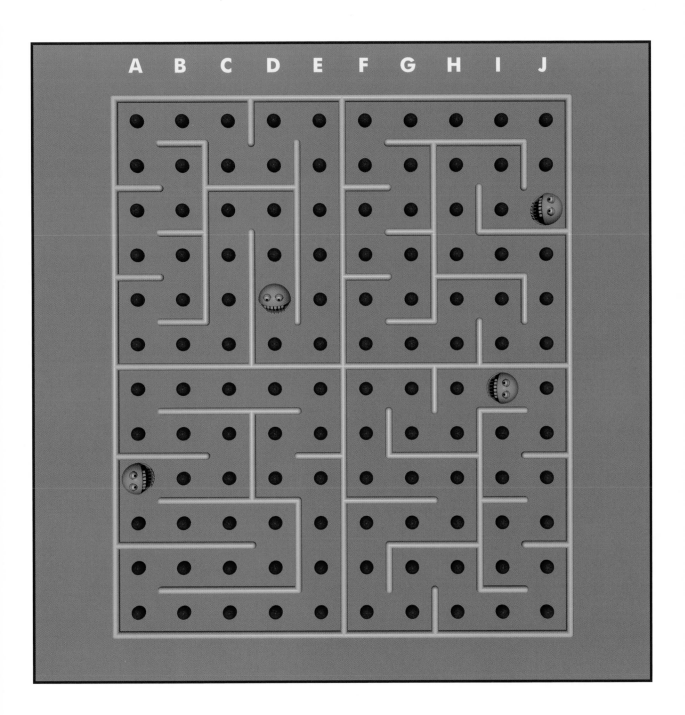

27 We put four trays atop one another. The trays are identical, but they are rotated differently. If we drop a ball into the top tray, which hole will it end up in?

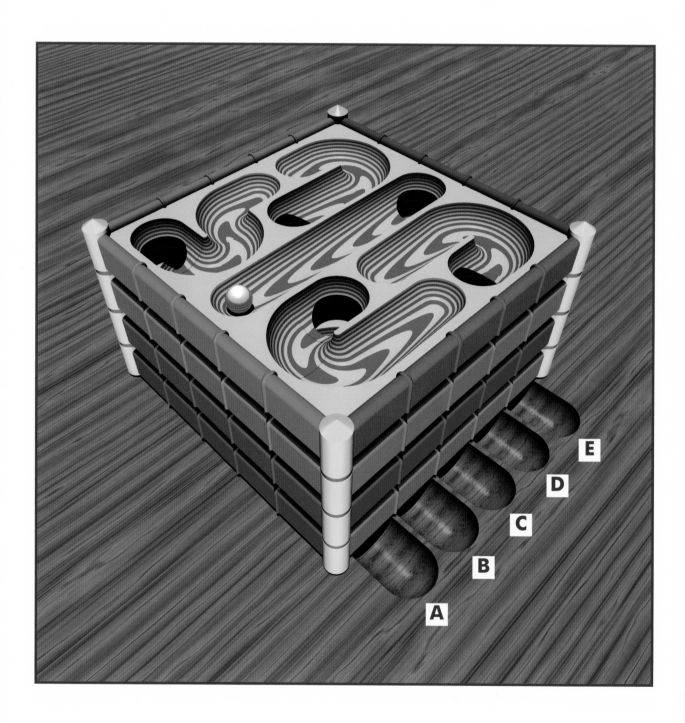

28 Most of these ships appear in four different colors, but four of them have only three colors. Can you find which ones?

Pair the shapes with their shadows.

1

2

3

4

A

B

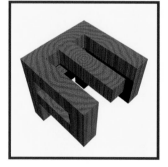
C

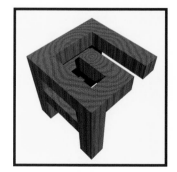
D

30 Which sticks can be pushed all the way through the green object?

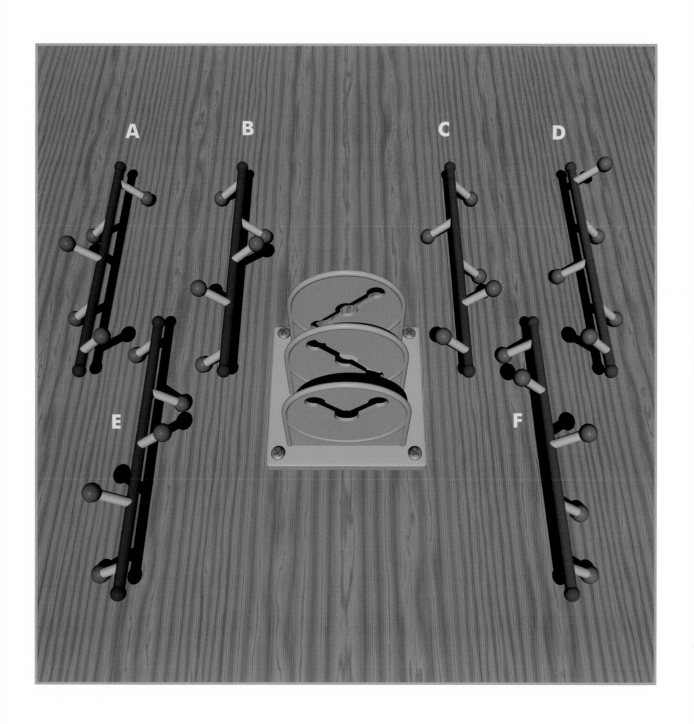

A

B

C

D

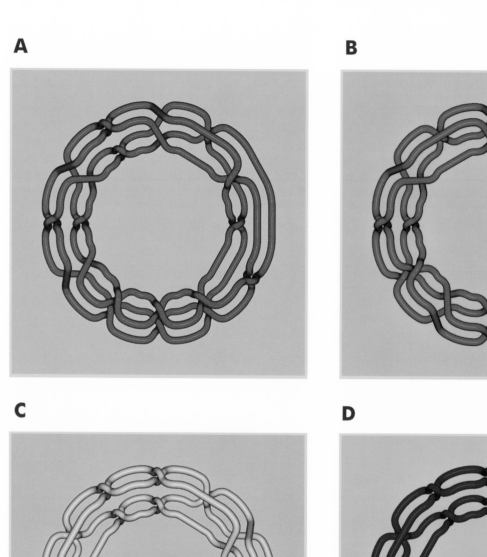

Collect all the marbles starting with the white one. You can remove a marble in a line if no others are between it and the one just removed. You can't go backward and can only turn on a marble.

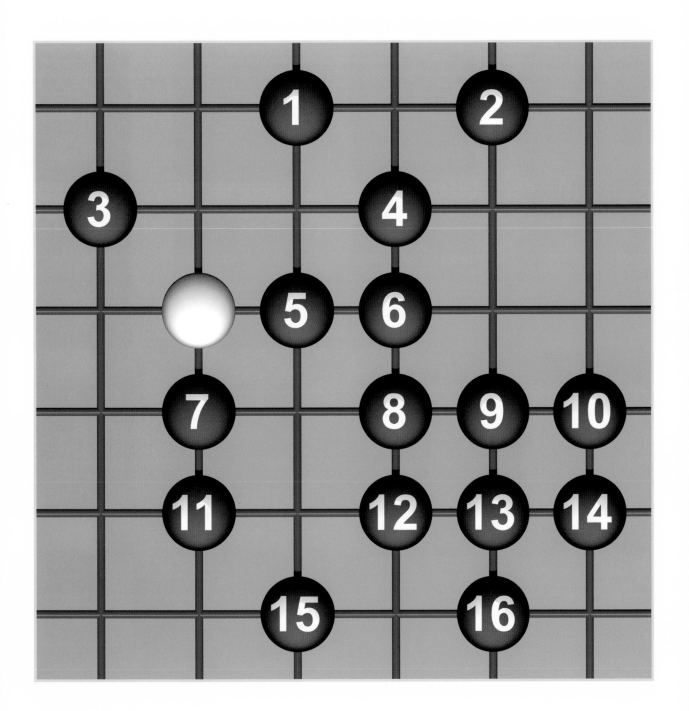

33 Find two identical pumpkin heads, then find the one whose eyes, nose, and mouth are different from the others in its row and column.

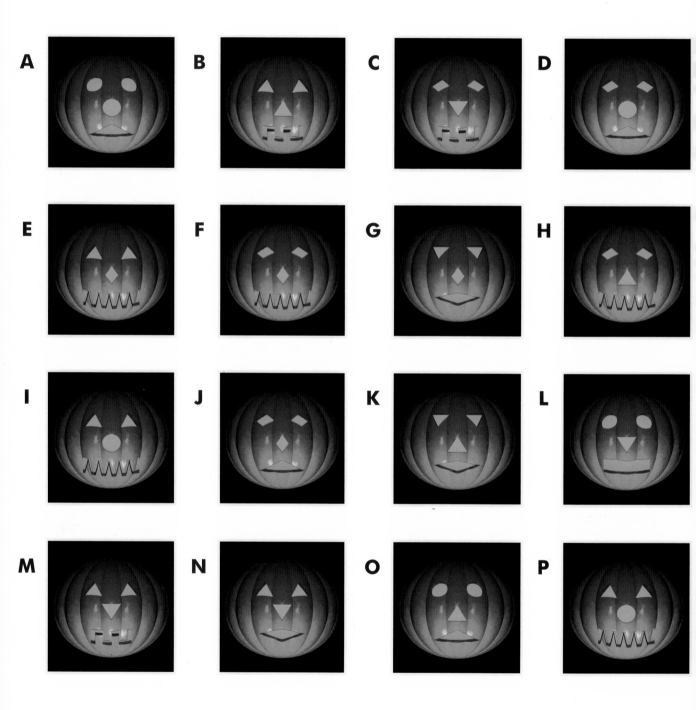

34 The picture shows special heat-sensitive matches that ignite only at their phosphoric end and only when there's fire near it. They burn at exactly the same rate. Which match will be the last to ignite if we light the blue one?

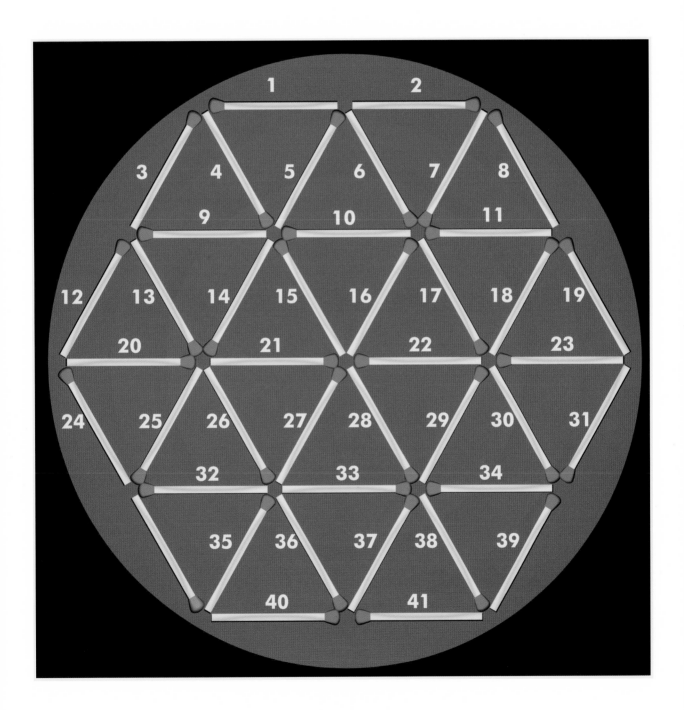

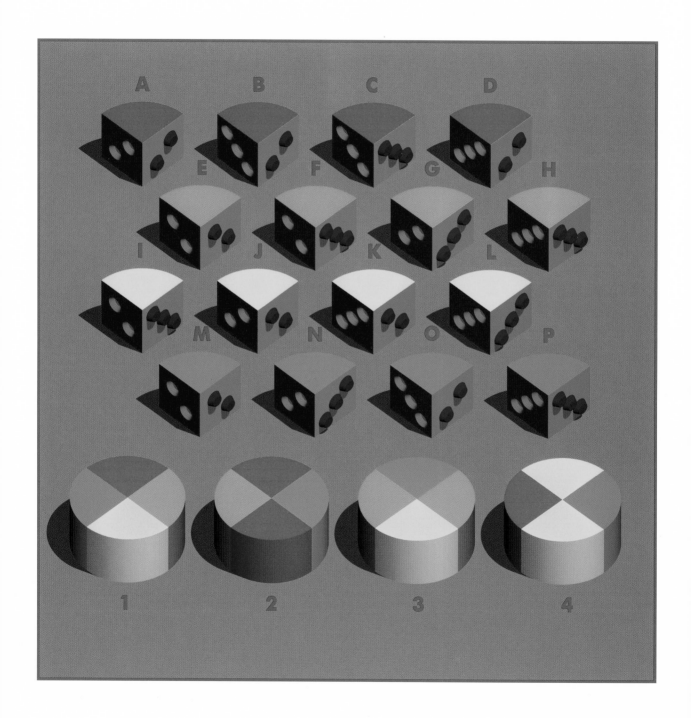

Which umbrella can be spotted in all four pictures?

37 Each red-and-yellow ribbon has eight holes. Pair the ribbons whose hole patterns are identical.

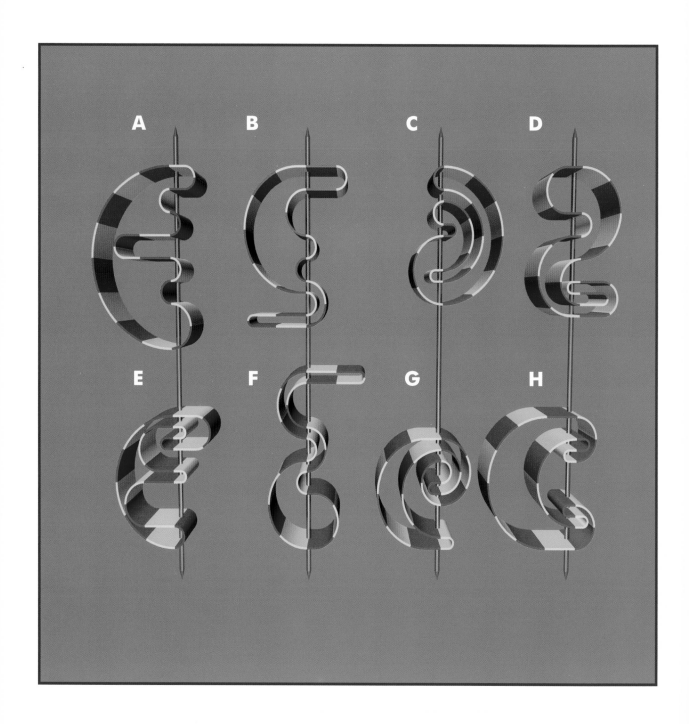

The mirror shows blocks with bulges on the one side and indentations on the other. Stack the blue blocks into a pile next to the green ones.

Pictured below are five different shapes. Four of them are seen from three different angles. The fifth is shown only once. Which one?

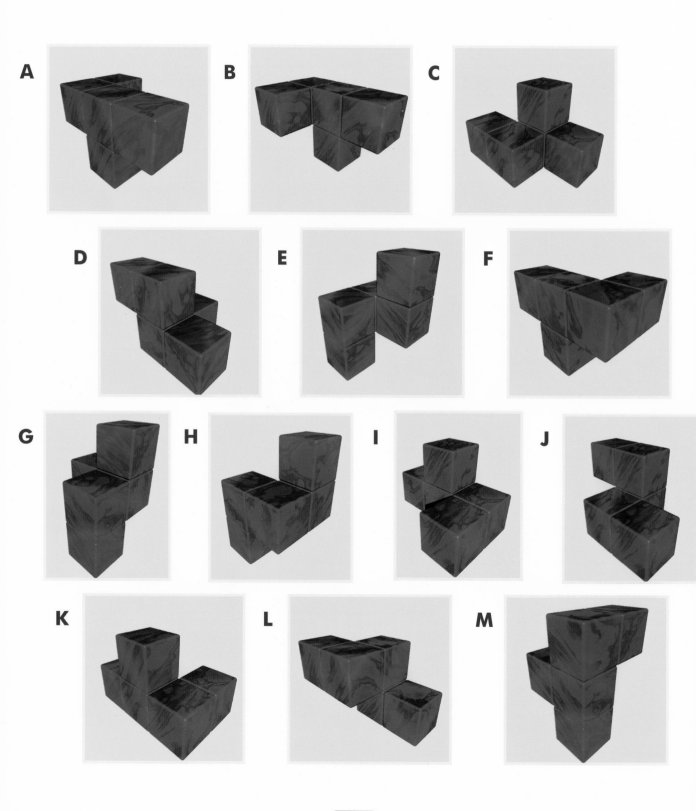

The three castle walls were built from the blocks in the upper left corner. Each wall contains all but one of the blocks. Can you find the missing one in each one?

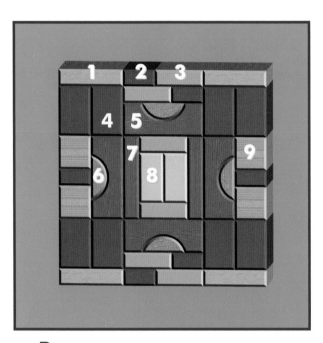

A

B

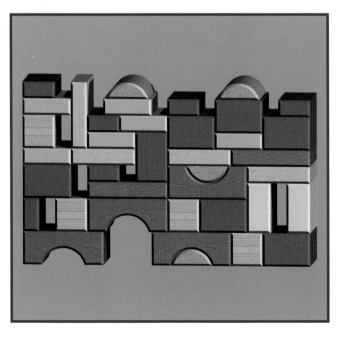

C

Which dominoes are in each column? Pair the standing dominoes with the numbered sets below them.

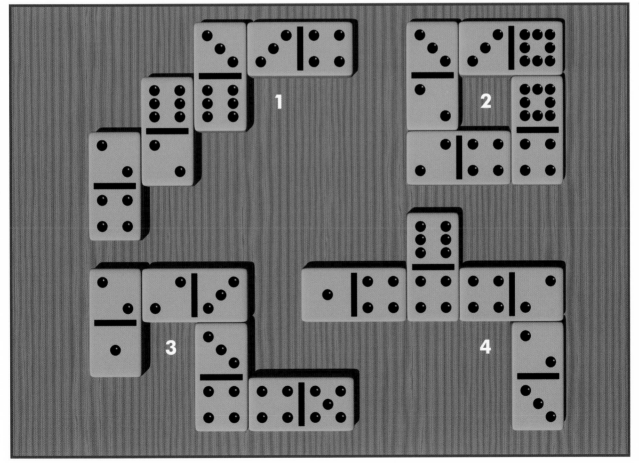

43 Pair the goblets with their mirror images.

The numbered shapes were built from the three components above them. What is the order of components from outermost to innermost?

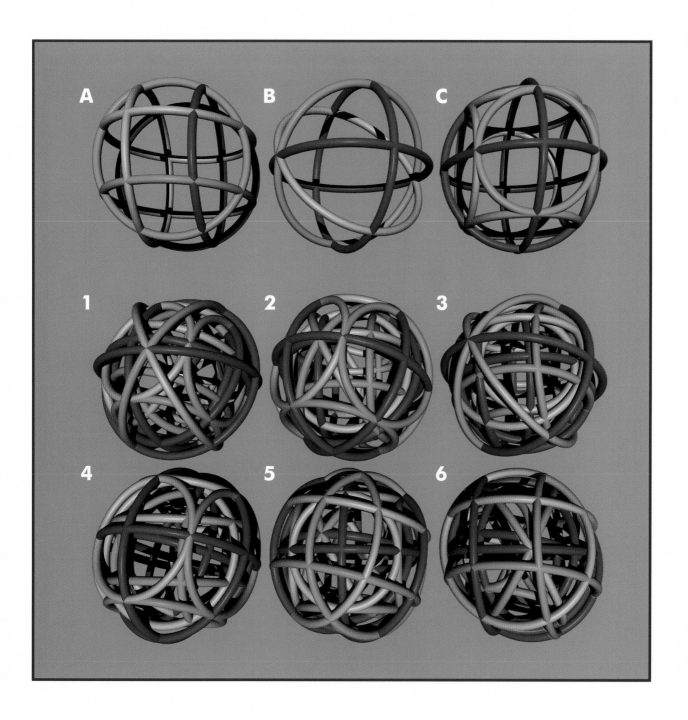

45 Each light is controlled by one of the switches, but we don't know which. We also don't know the on and off positions of the switches. Study the first three pictures to figure out the switch positions in the fourth.

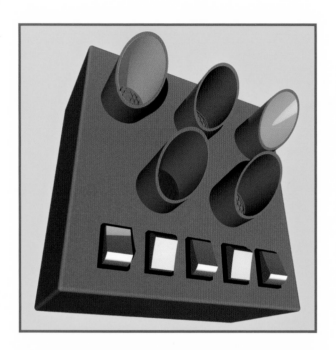

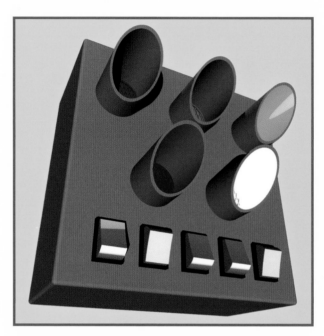

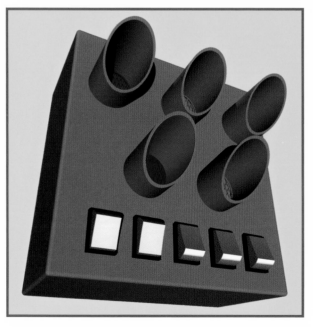

46 Move each piece by jumping the number of steps the arrow indicates (the color code is above the board). Jump in the direction of the arrow the piece is on. Which piece reaches the middle first?

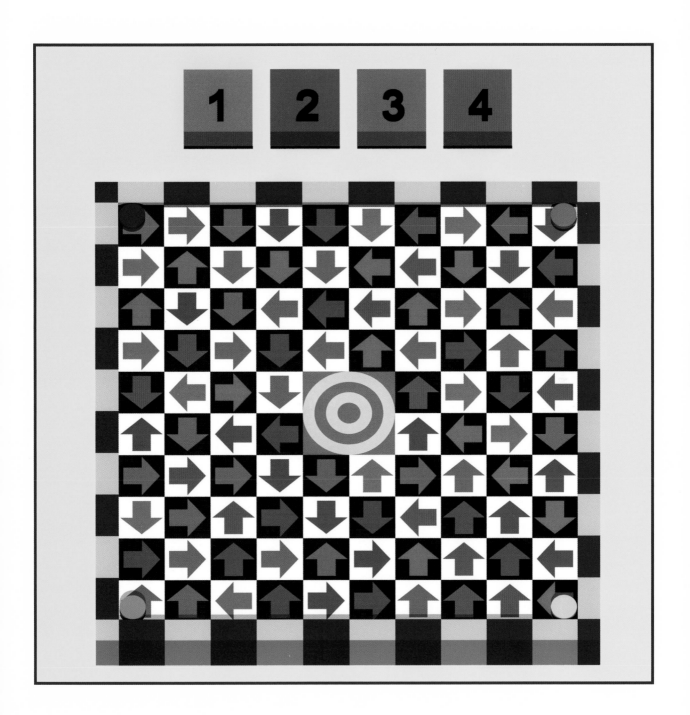

47 We twisted five ribbons, then squashed them. Pair off the pictures made before and after.

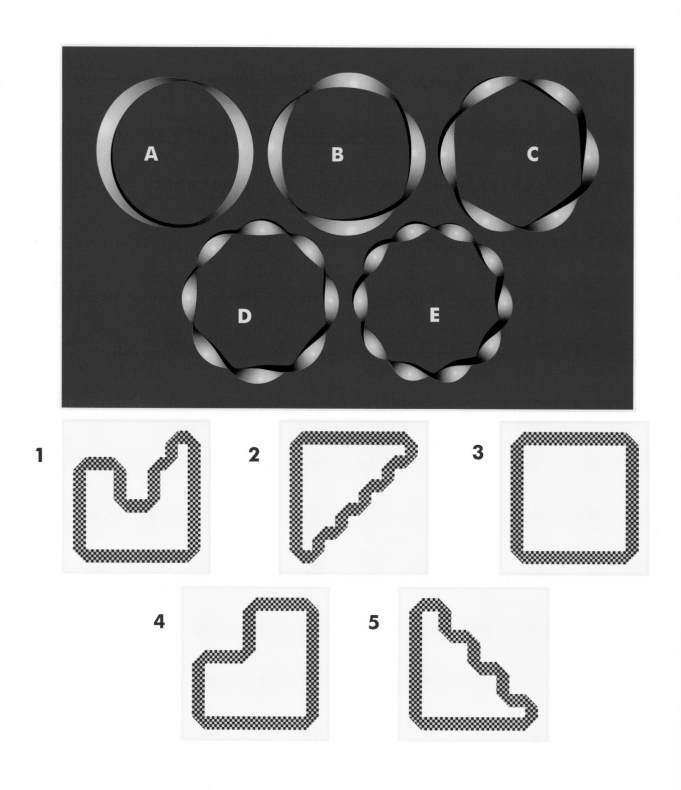

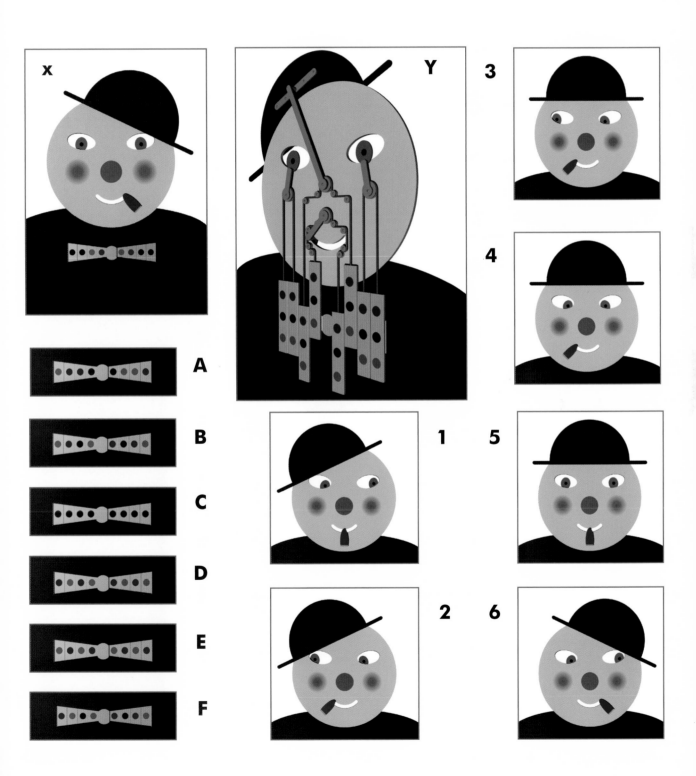

Study the two balanced scales. How many red balls are needed to balance the third one? (Balls of the same color are identical in weight.)

Build the shape in the middle using all nine puzzle pieces.

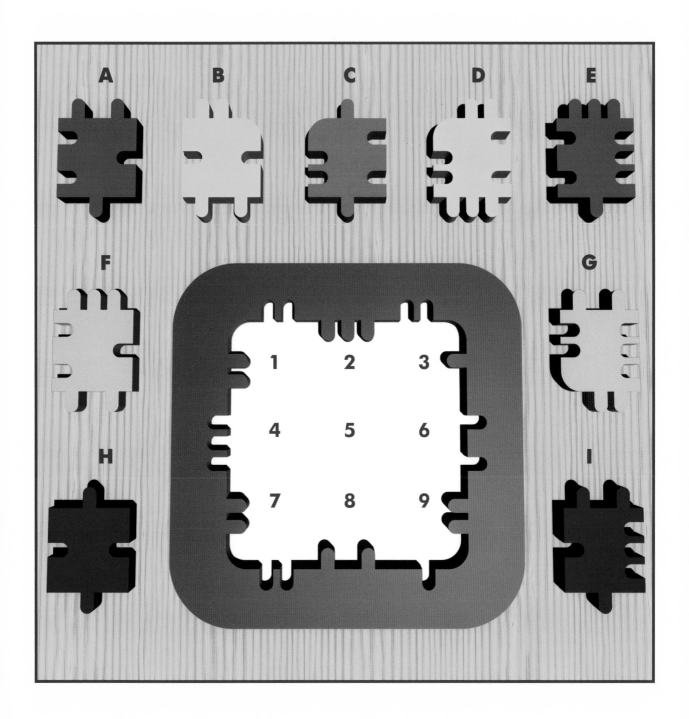

51 Which aerial view shows the velocipedes accurately?

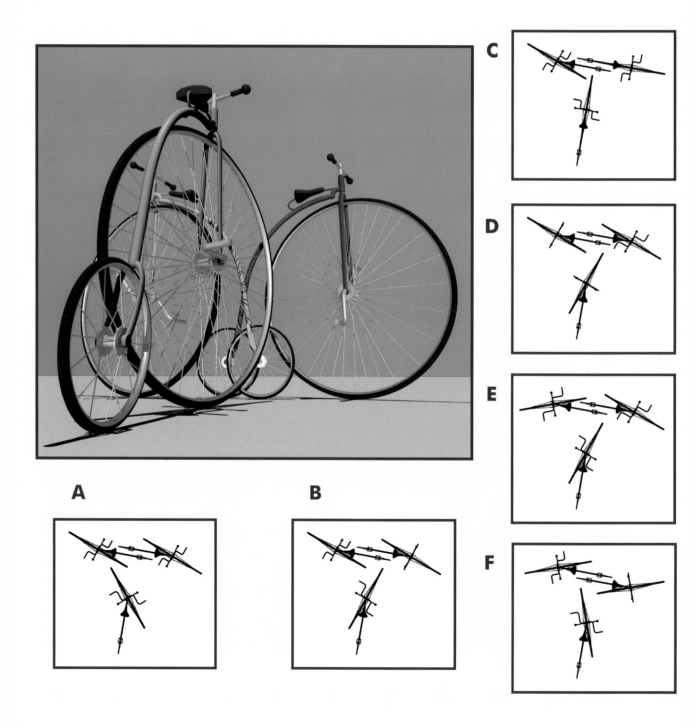

A

B

C

D

E

F

A

B

C

D

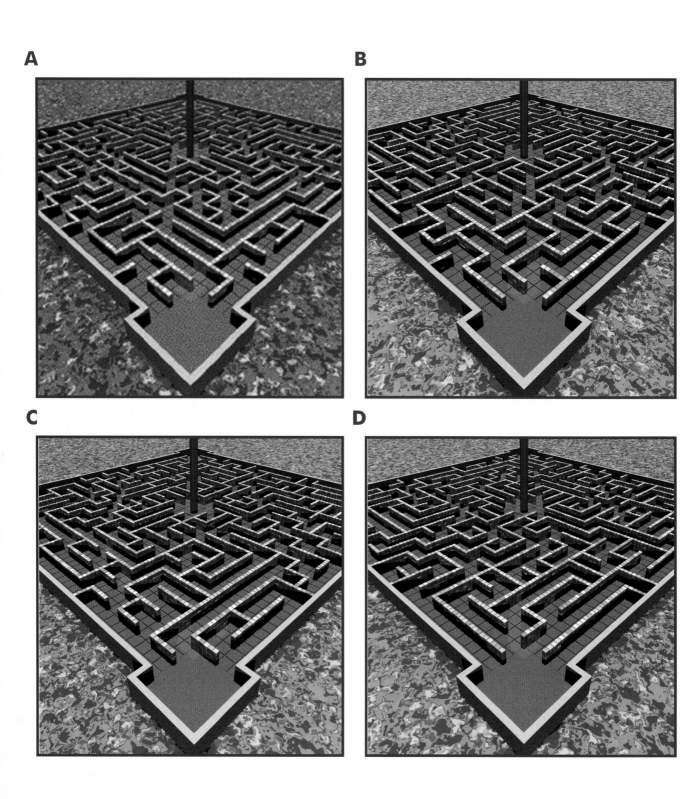

Pair the pictures that show the same object from the top and side.

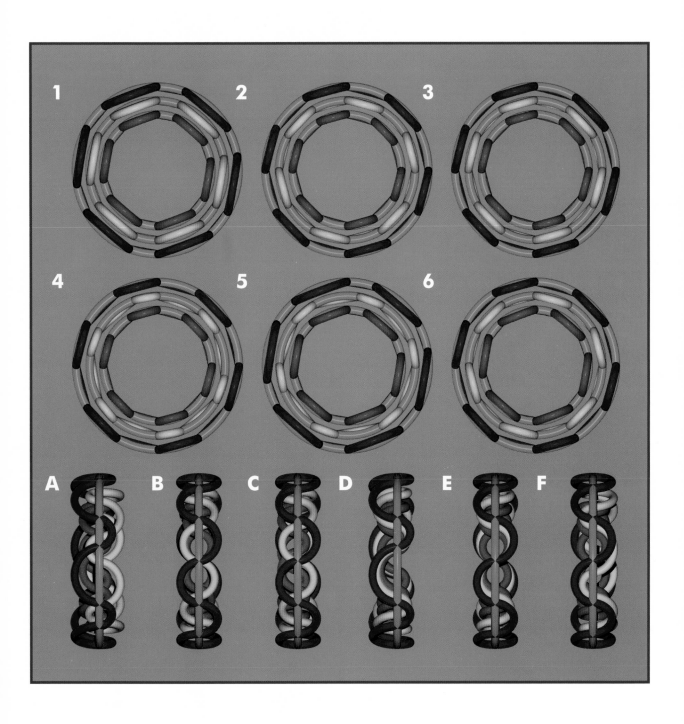

In what order did we place the billiard balls if the distance between any two successively placed balls decreases?

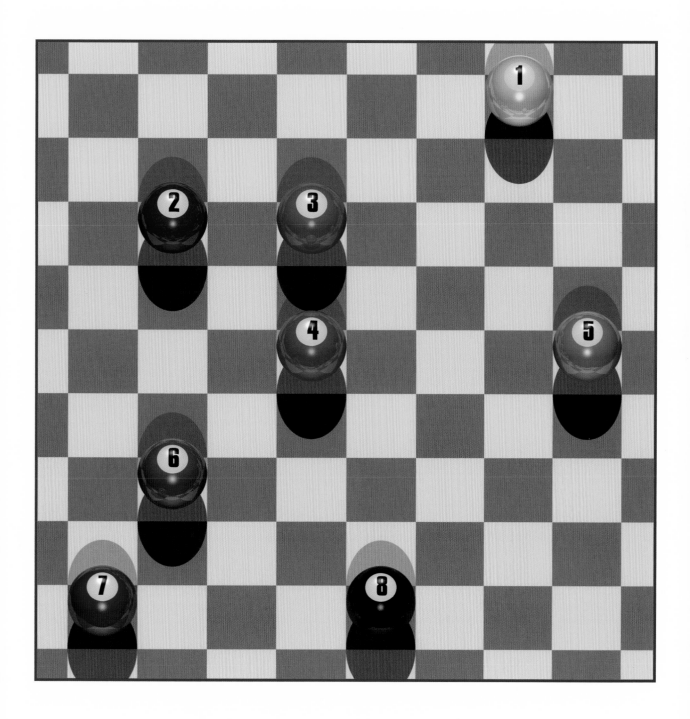

A

C

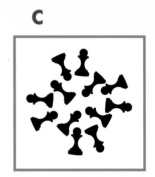

B

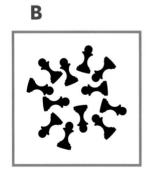

D

The pictures show the inside and outside of a safe. How many times should we turn the handle to open the door?

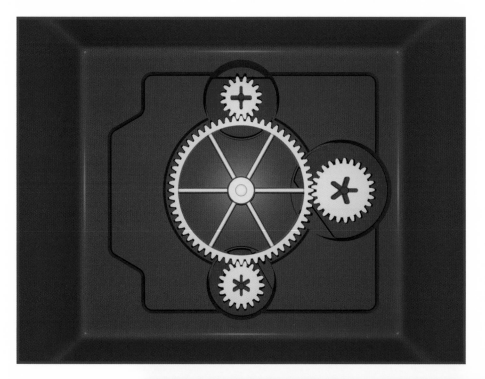

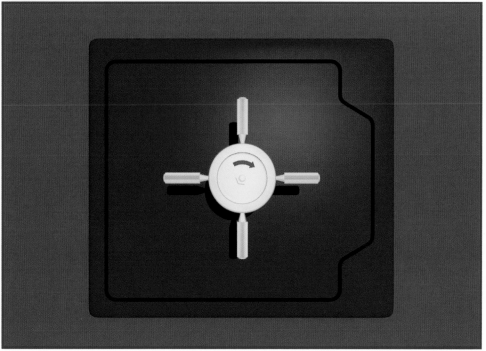

59 Four small monsters ramble along their labyrinths at the same speed. They never turn back and they gobble up every circle along the way. Which vertical column will be emptied first?

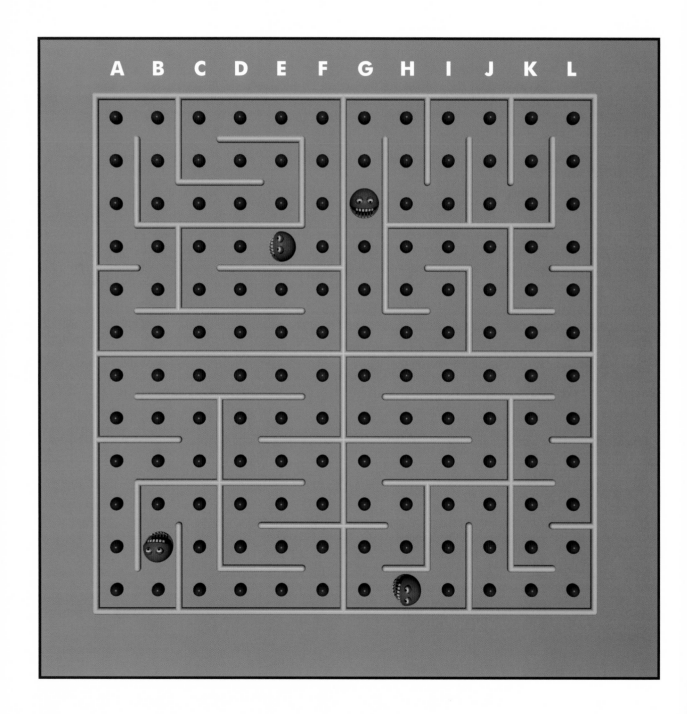

60 Arrange the pieces on the numbered areas to make a closed pipeline.

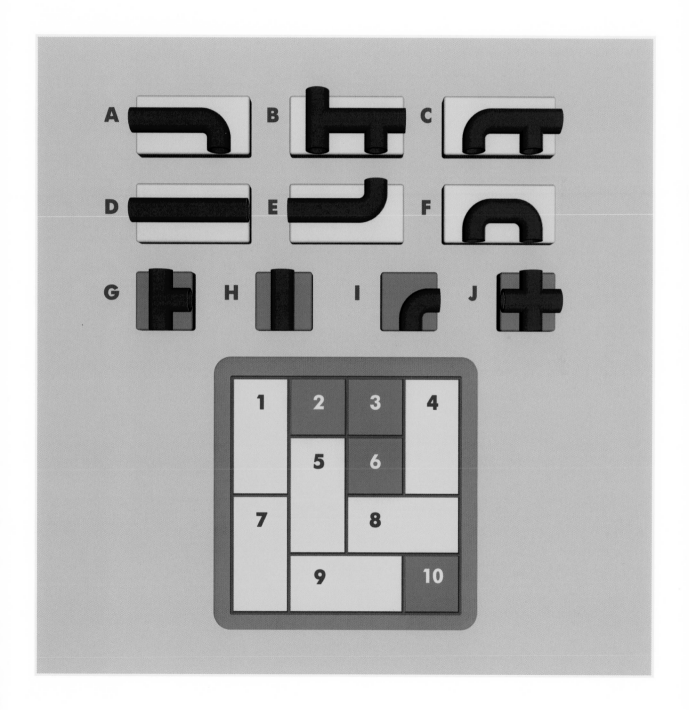

This balanced structure is made up from 1, 2, 3, 4, and 5 kilogram pieces. Pair the weights with the pieces.

A

B

E

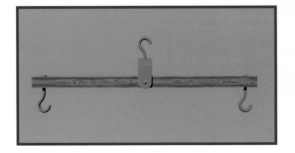

D

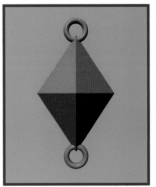

C

Study the color scheme and arrange the points of the star.

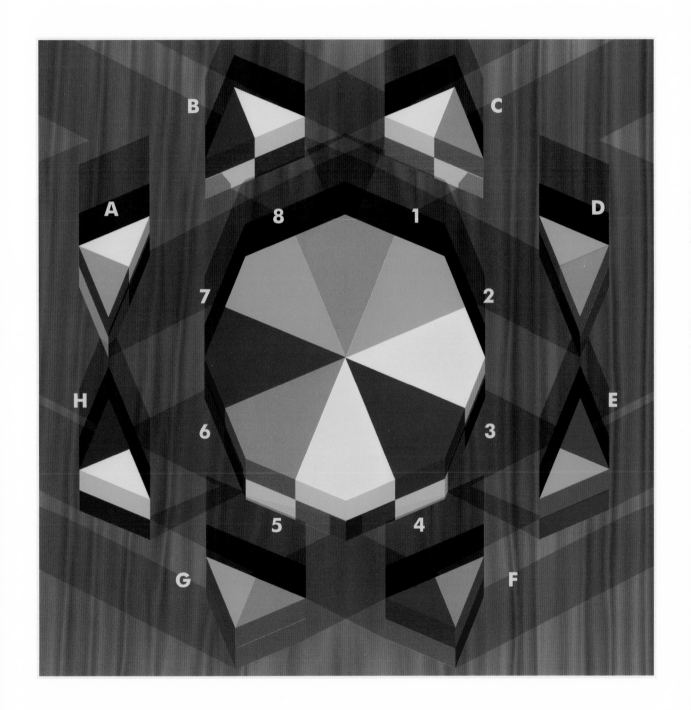

63 Pair the figures with their views from the bottom.

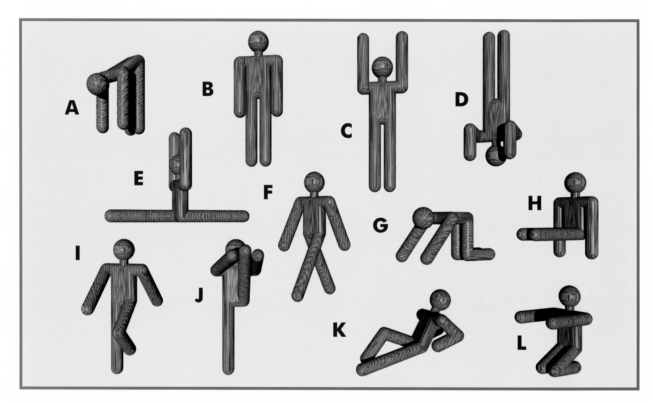

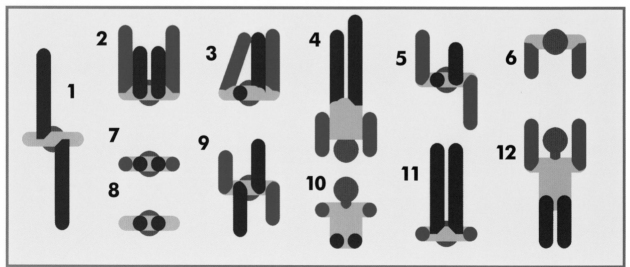

64 These pictures show six magic cubes from two different angles. Pair the pictures that show the same cube.

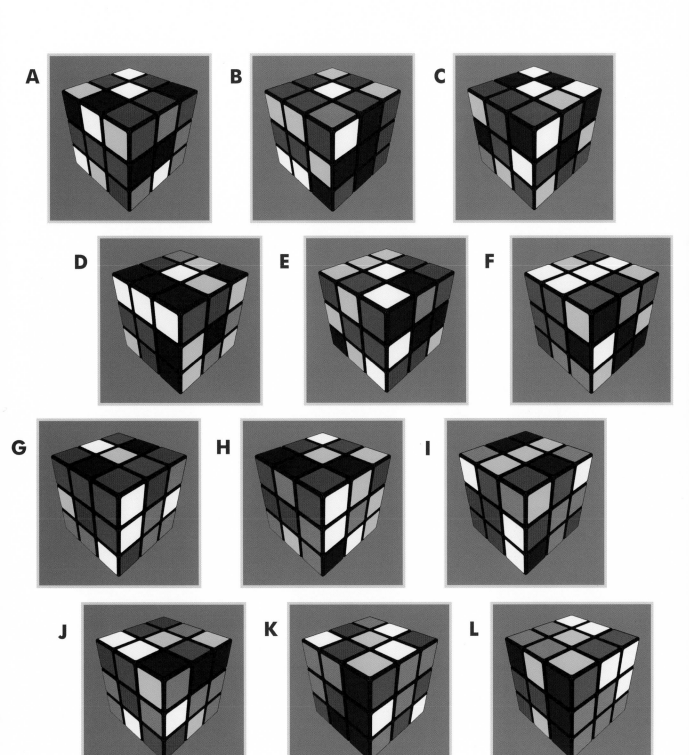

65 Pair off the pyramids with their aerial views.

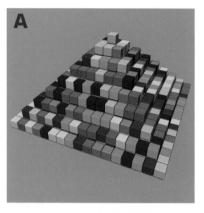

A

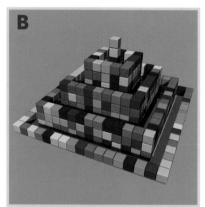

B

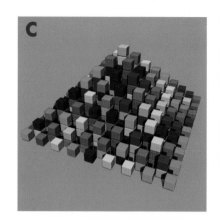

C

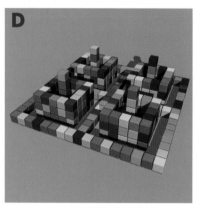

D

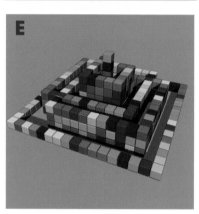

E

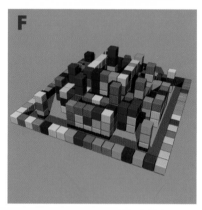

F

1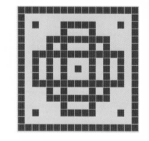

2

3

4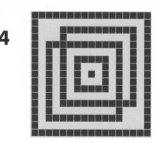

5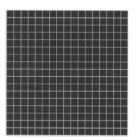

6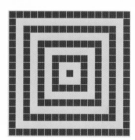

The springs extend in direct proportion to the weight on them. Which structure will extend the farthest? (Rods and springs weigh the same.)

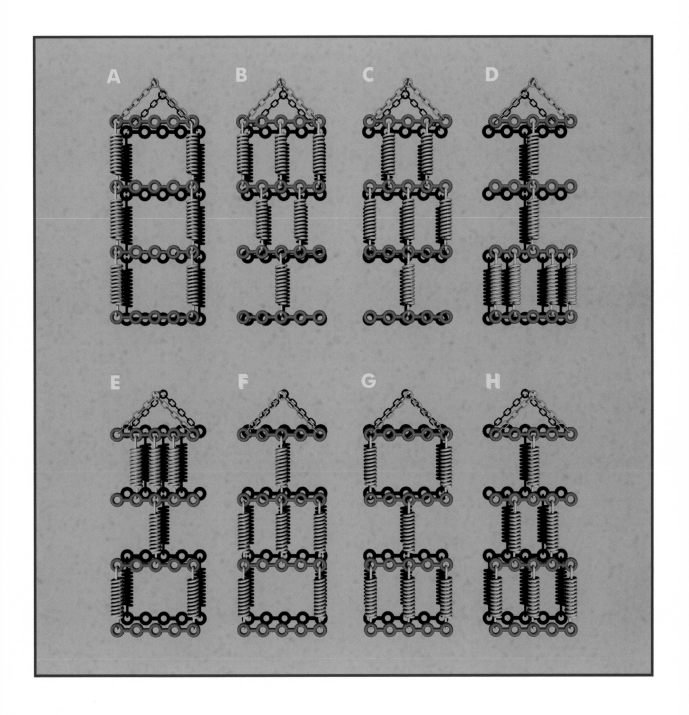

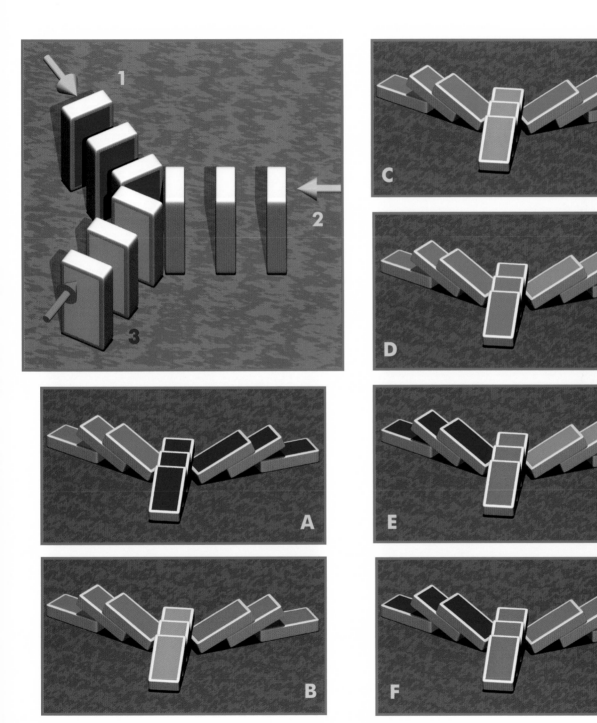

Each time we took a picture of the bears sitting down, one of them turned her head. Can you spot which one in each picture?

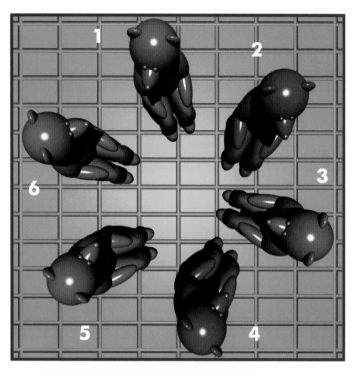

A

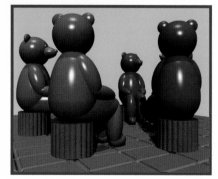

B

C

D

E

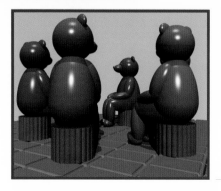

F

The shapes at the top were created from the components shown in the middle. Pair the shapes with their numbered footprints.

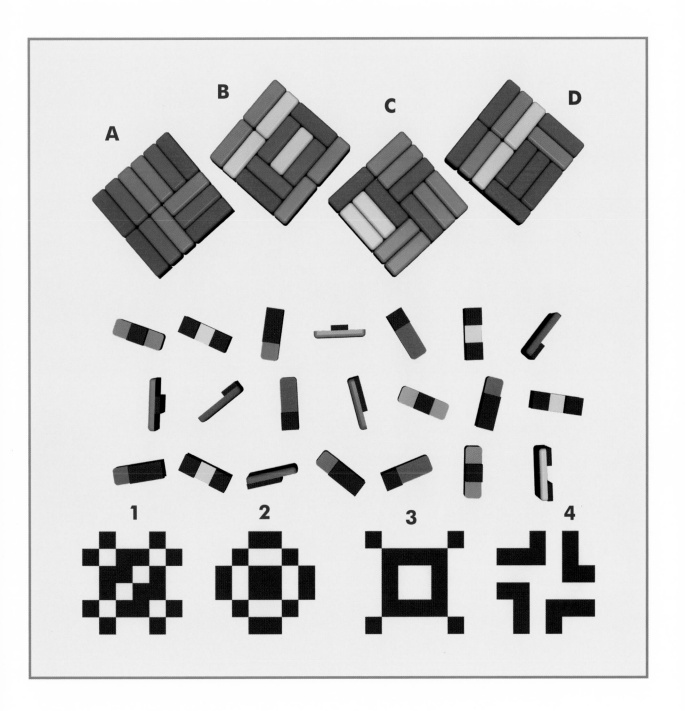

The letters mark areas where the vases fell and broke. Pair the broken pieces at the bottom with the lettered areas.

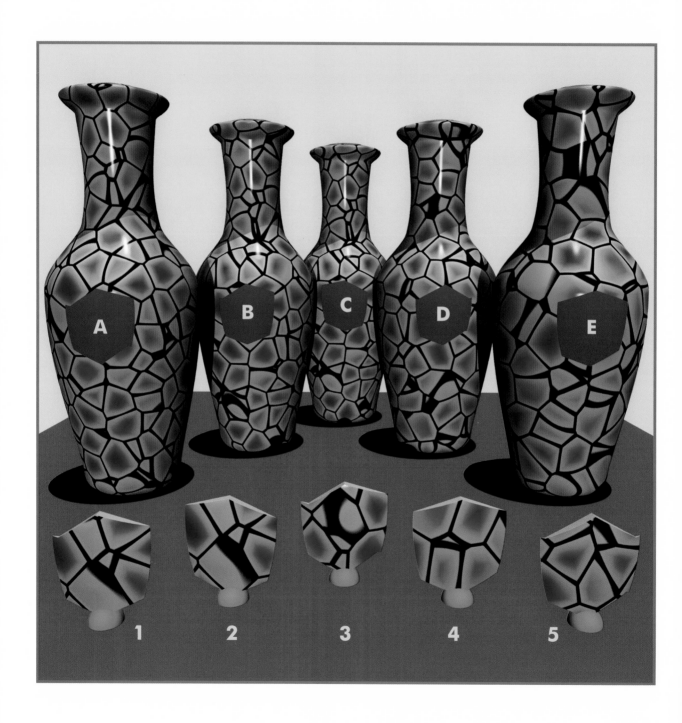

On the magic cube, red is opposite orange, green is opposite blue, and white is opposite yellow. We turned the faces 90 degrees five times. Pictures A–F show where the individual colors are. We have substituted patterns for colors. Can you determine the colors?

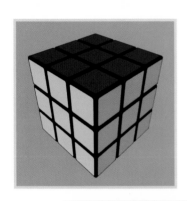

1

2

3

4

5

A

B

C

D

E

F

Pair the keys with the impressions of their edges.

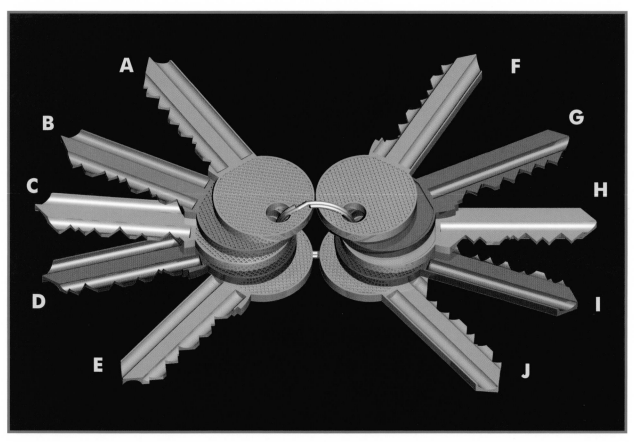

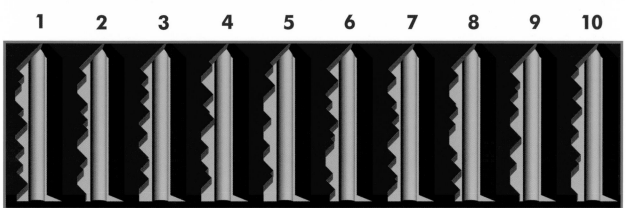

In what order can we pull the shapes out of the box?

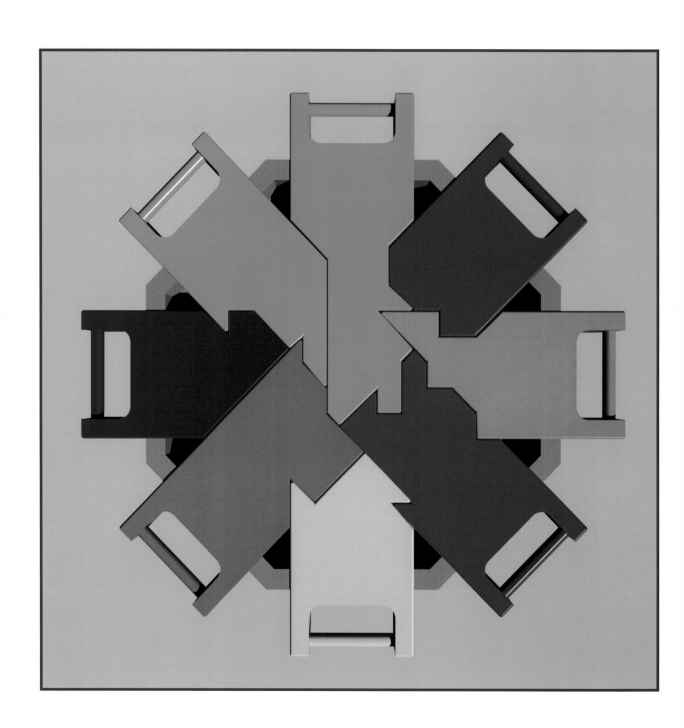

Collect all the stones, starting from the first one. You can only pick up a stone if the previous one pointed at it.

Which six shapes must be connected, and how, to make a ring?

In what order should we pick up the stones if the distance between two successively collected stones is increasing?

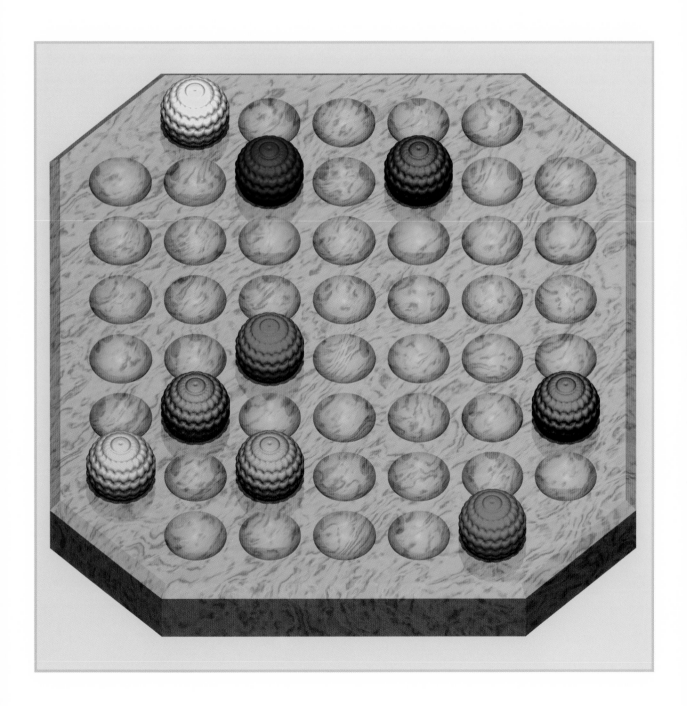

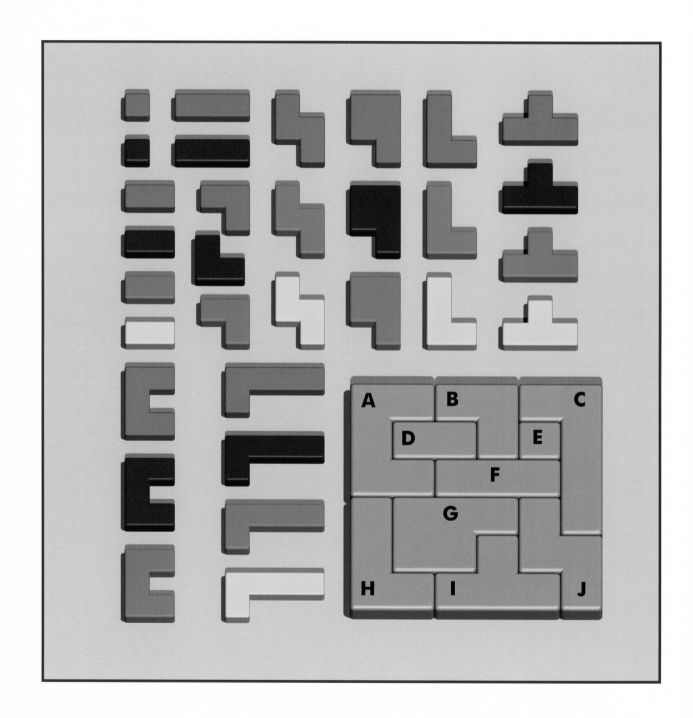

80 In which cases can we collect all the tokens using the knight's move (from chess)?

A

B

C

D

E

F
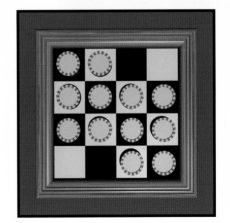

If the hour hands and the minute hands of clocks B, D, and F are extended, they create a triangle. How much time elapses until the same happens with any three clocks?

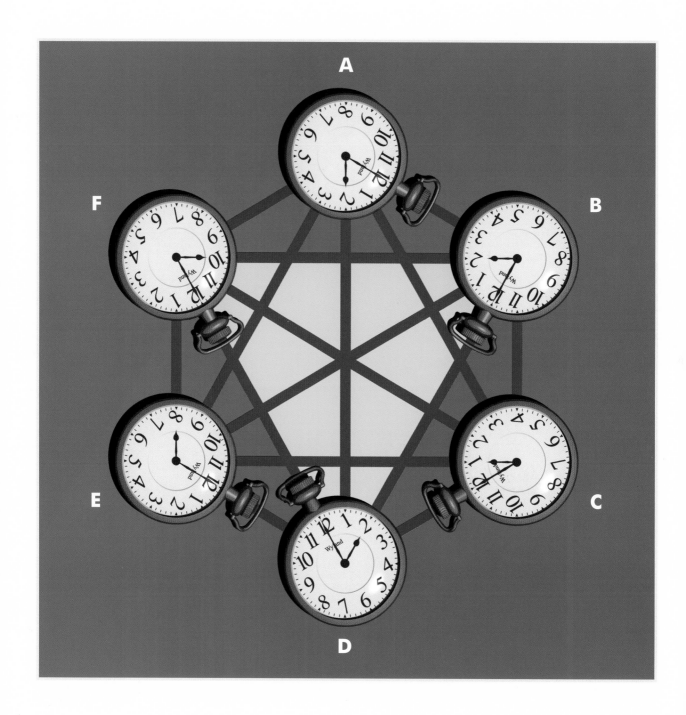

What is inscribed on the Japanese stamps? Pair the letters with the numbers.

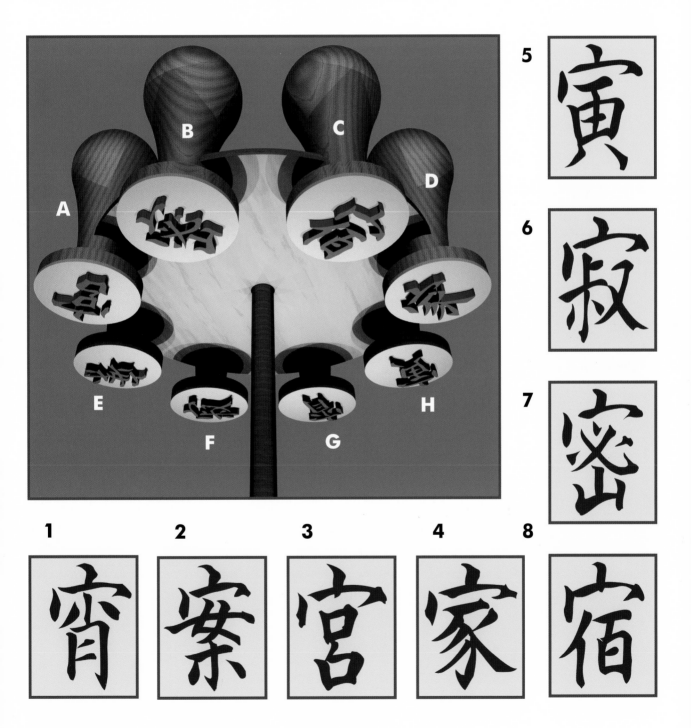

83 Replace the white stones with black ones so that in each line the numbers on the stones add up to 26.

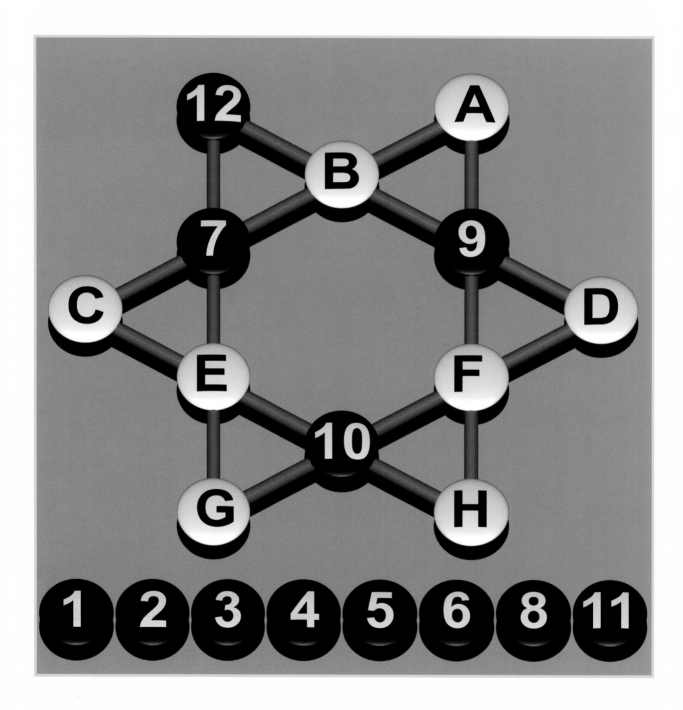

Study the three balanced scales. How many yellow balls are needed to balance the fourth one? (Balls of the same color weigh the same.)

A

B

C

D

85 **Where did the slices originally belong?**

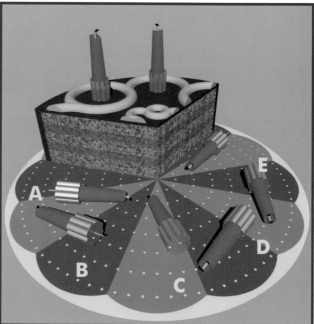

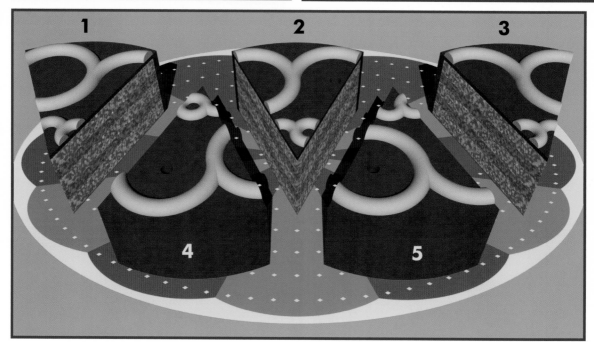

86 The picture shows an archipelago. Which four red buoys should be replaced with a lighthouse if we want to light all the white portions of the sea, no matter how tall the buildings on the islands are?

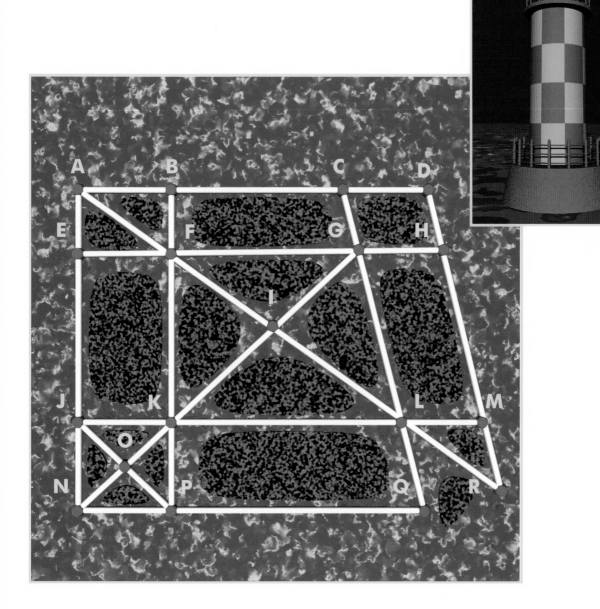

1. A–D (11 units), B–F (9 units), C–G (10 units), E–H (8 units).

2. B. Configuration A expands to 7: B to 9; C and D each to 6.

3. 5. The top two cubes each have 1 on the bottom and 6 on top. The second from the bottom has 3 on the bottom and 4 on top. The bottom cube has 5 on the bottom and 2 on top.

4. C. The longest continuous black-white series in A is 14 pearls; in B, is 12; in C, 20; and in D, 18.

5. A–3, B–4, C–1, D–2.

6. Brown, yellow, green, violet, orange, red, blue, cyan.

7. A–3, B–1, C–2.

8. Purple, yellow, red, blue, aqua, green.

9. 1–B, 2–A, 3–D, 4–C.

10. First box: 4–5–7, second box: 2–3–8, third box: 1–6–9.

11. 1: H–4, 2: E–2, 3: C–7, 4: B–1, 5: F–6, 6: D–4.

12. A–2, B–3, C–4, D–1.

13. F–K.

14. 3.

15. A–E, B–H, C–I, D–J, F–G, K–L.

16. 1–D, 2–B, 3–C, 4–F, 5–E, 6–A.

17. A–B, C–I, D–G, E–J, H–L, F–K.

18. A–1, B–3, C–2, D–5, E–4, F–6.

19. 1: B+E, 2: G+H, 3: A+C, 4: D+F.

20. 1–E, 2–A, 3–B, 4–D, 5–C, 6–E.

21. A–G, B–F, C–J, D–H, E–I.

22. A–3, B–1, C–2, D–4, E–6, F–5.

23. A, J, L, F, D, K, E, C, N, G, M, O, B, H, I, P.

24. D.

25. The blue light must be turned on. The second switch from the left controls the white light, and the fourth controls the green. It is unclear which switch controls the blue light and which the red, but based on the two positions, blue is on and red is off.

26. E.

27. A.

28. White sailboat (like the second from the left, row two), blue canoe (like the third from the left, row two), green ocean liner (like the third from the left, row one), and yellow pirate ship (like the rightmost one, row one).

29. 1–D, 2–B, 3–C, 4–A.

30. B, C, E.

31. A–3, B–2, C–1, D–4.

32. White, 5, 6, 8, 9, 2, 1, 15, 16, 13, 14, 10, 7, 11, 12, 4, 3.

33. I and P , L.

34. 38. First unit: blue-headed; second unit: 25, 32; third unit: 13, 14, 20, 26, 35; fourth unit: 4, 9, 10, 12, 15, 24; fifth unit: 1, 3, 6, 7, 11, 16, 21, 22, 27; sixth unit: 2, 5, 8, 17, 18, 19, 23, 29; seventh unit: 28, 33, 34, 37; eighth unit: 30, 31, 36, 39, 40, 41; ninth unit: 38.

35. C–H–K–N, D–M–A–F, O–E–J–G, I–P–L–B.

36. The green-and-black umbrella with eight segments.

37. A–H, B–G, C–E, D–F.

38. E–C–B–D–F–A.

39. A–K–M, B–F–I, C–D–G, E–J–L. Shape H is unpaired.

40. Third from the left, second shelf from the top; left outermost, second shelf from the bottom.